EPIC

MEDITERRANEAN diet COOKBOOK

LORENZ BLONT

INTRODUCTION

The eating propensities of the rustic populace within the Mediterranean between 1950 and 1960 coined the term "Mediterranean slim down." Mother Nature conveyed the nourishment for this earnestly plant-based eat less free of charge. Individuals ate what the locale had to offer in seasons, such as new natural product and vegetables, rice, potatoes, nuts, the popular pasta, and bounty of olive oil. There were moreover barbecued angle and a glass of ruddy wine. For numerous a long time the occupants cooked like this, particularly within the olive-growing zones on Crete, Greece, and Italy, and were for the most part in fabulous wellbeing. Since the entry of quick nourishment and ready-made items in Southern Europe, the tide has turned.

The conventional Mediterranean count calories is as it were arranged absolutely because it used to be in some little areas. The Mediterranean diet's establishment is vegetables, natural products, herbs, nuts, beans, and entire grains. Dinners are built around these plant-based nourishments. Direct sums of dairy, poultry, and eggs are moreover central to the Mediterranean Eat less, as is fish. In differentiate, ruddy meat is eaten as it were occasionally. Since the climatic conditions and taste inclinations shift significantly in numerous southern nations, there's no uniform Mediterranean slim down within the Mediterranean locale. However, similitudes can be found in selecting and planning the nourishments that are characteristic of conventional Mediterranean cooking. In any case, it could be a adjusted and shifted eat less that gives an expansive number of profitable fixings for wellbeing. Tender cooking, such as stewing or steaming, guarantees that these are barely misplaced amid cooking.

Heart malady, corpulence, diabetes and cancer are comparatively uncommon within the whole Mediterranean locale. In expansion to solid dinners, which moreover incorporate a glass of wine, the slower pace of life likely moreover plays a vital part. The mystery has not however been completely uncovered, but it is undisputed that the individuals around the Mediterranean advantage from the assorted new, regular items of their country - the frequently greatly handled nourishments of the worldwide nourishment industry are still the special case here "If you need simple, delicious and inexpensive recipes to form, this is often the cookbook for you! Each formula we have attempted and has been superb. It takes exceptionally small time to collect the formulas and not many ingredients. The fixings are very common and what you'd as of now have in your pantry." Usually a portion of an awfully cited audit that appears what the foremost common require for a formula book is, and my book and formulas must adhere for the major portion to it.

Fried fish and vegetables with a view of the sea - most people probably think that is a dream. Eating like you're on vacation sounds promising, doesn't it? The

Mediterranean Diet is based on exactly this principle and looks our southern European neighbors on the plate. Find out what is behind the Mediterranean diet, how and if it works here!

Mediterranean Diet

An adjusted, solid, shifted, and top notch eat less is the premise of the Mediterranean eat less. Here, the propensities of the Mediterranean are adopted. However, the Mediterranean eat less isn't a genuine eat less, but or maybe a frame of nourishment and a way of life in which fiber-rich blended nourishments and new fixings are on the menu. Too, care is taken to guarantee that person suppers are eaten gradually and comfortably.

A moderate weight misfortune of two kilos per month is guaranteed. The concept is more of a solid eat less than a slim down. To lose weight, you ought to number calories and utilize olive oil sparingly. The Mediterranean slim down is stylish since it is tasty and solid. That's why we illuminate you nowadays approximately the basic nuts and bolts of the Mediterranean eat less, one of the foremost useful shapes of nutrition worldwide. Find the foremost critical things nowadays so that you, simply as well can appreciate all the benefits of this eat less.

7 Reason to Get Started

The Mediterranean nourishment is exceptionally well known around the world since of its numerous wellbeing benefits. At that point, we go into the foremost critical preferences and viewpoints of this top-notch shape of nutrition:

1. Decreased chance of cardiovascular disease A ponder by the Harvard TH Chan School of Open Wellbeing appears that the Mediterranean eat less can reduce the hazard of cardiovascular illness by 25% over the next 12 a long time since this may lower terrible cholesterol (LDL).
2. Longer life This comes about of a consider by the Harvard School of Open Wellbeing. The College of Athens Restorative School appears that the Mediterranean slim down drags out life.

3. Conceivably advantageous in anticipating cognitive decline the comes about of a ponder from 2015 demonstrate that more seasoned individuals who eat a Mediterranean slim down may encounter a change in their mental capacities. Another piece of investigating too concluded that the Mediterranean count calories might moderate down the untimely improvement of Alzheimer's.

4. Conceivably, security from cancer in 2017, analysts found that individuals who take after tall Mediterranean diets are less likely to create cancer, particularly colon cancer. There was too a slight lessening in breast cancer frequencies.

5. Direct utilization of ruddy meat Since ruddy meat can cause well-being issues, it is best to devour it in balance. The immersed fats contained in it ought to be eaten every so often within the Mediterranean diet.

6. Mediterranean Slim down: Dairy items each day Yogurt and cheese can moreover be found in Mediterranean cooking. They give essential minerals such as calcium and phosphorus, as well as vitamins and high-quality proteins.

7. Mediterranean slim down and exercise A definite eat less ought to be supplemented with adequate work out to be sound and fit. So do not disregard to exercise every day to induce the foremost out of the Mediterranean eat less.

Exchanging to the Mediterranean count calories is more often than not exceptionally troublesome. There are numerous delightful dishes with the prescribed nourishments, and it could be a very flexible count calorie. It is best to urge a nutritionist to donate your tips and specify nourishment arrange extraordinarily outlined for you.

Pyramid of Mediterranean recipe

Nourishment pyramids are utilized to allot macronutrients to particular categories. Whereby you ought to as it expended little sums of nourishment at the beat of the pyramid. Items within the center or at the foot of the pyramid are appropriate for direct or huge quantities. In the case of the Mediterranean slim down, desserts and meat tend to be at the best of the nourishment pyramid. In contrast, poultry and dairy items can be delighted in indirect amounts and angles, natural products, vegetables, entirety grain items and different oils in huge quantities.

The Mediterranean diet is among the most excellent in terms of varying wellbeing perspectives. For illustration, it is one of the foremost compelling and most advantageous diets for moving forward cardiovascular health. The most imperative highlights of the Mediterranean eat less are moo fat admissions, mainly soaked greasy acids (e.g., rosy meat, butter, etc.), visit utilization of fish and angle, expanded entries of carbohydrates (cereal items, vegetables, natural product, vegetables and drain) and the tall utilization of olive oil

The Mediterranean eat less is wealthy in vitamins, follow components, and fundamental greasy acids (linoleic corrosive, α- and γ-linolenic corrosive and arachidic acid).

QUESTIONS AND ANSWERS ON MEDITERRANEAN RECIPES

Q1. What are ordinary Mediterranean vegetables? The cooking from the Mediterranean locale is considered exceptionally solid, not the slightest sense of the Mediterranean vegetables, expanding to auberges, zucchini, peppers, and tomatoes. These incorporate artichokes and olives, broccoli, beans and onions, and garlic. Also, celery, spinach, carrots, mushrooms, and different leaf servings of mixed greens such as radicchio can be portrayed as ordinary Mediterranean vegetables.

In most cases, the conclusive figure is the composition of new fixings and new herbs. The various fresh herbs from the Mediterranean locale such as basil, rosemary, thyme, oregano, sage, mint, and inlet leaf circular off the dishes' taste. Mediterranean vegetables are frequently utilized in dishes with angle or fish. Ruddy meat is used sparingly.

An adjusted count of calories with parts of new Mediterranean vegetables and herbs, hook, fish, olives, and small meat can positively impact the cholesterol level and the cardiovascular system.

Q2. What makes a dish Mediterranean? Mediterranean nourishment ordinarily comprises a parcel of vegetables, natural products, and fish. These are all nourishments that contain numerous essential fixings. Those who take after a Mediterranean slim down doesn't take after a strict slim down arrange. Or maybe, Mediterranean cooking is a collection and concentration of eating propensities within the more prominent locale around the Mediterranean. The Mediterranean site is isolated from the connecting territory in regions.

These can be political, social, and, overall, climatological. In common, the area in which olive trees are planted is alluded to as the Mediterranean - it is the so-called olive tree line. Fundamentally, Mediterranean nourishment implies a combination of eating propensities and way of life. The last-mentioned plays a not inconsequential part and is comparable to the positive effects of wear. Individuals within the Mediterranean range eat natural products, vegetables, nuts, beans, and grain products.

Q3. What is the contrast between juice and smoothie? Juice may be fluid from a plant without fiber or mash. We drink juices since they are trustworthy. When we crush a liquid, the filaments and mash are misplaced, and with them a few of the proteins. This implies that our bodies do not process the juice to assimilate the supplements since they go straight into our bloodstream. You'll be able to crush juice from any plant. So, from natural products, vegetables, or herbs. A smoothie could be a drink based on fixings that are blended. This implies that the fixings are made fluid, whereas protecting the filaments and mash. Since they are made little, but not devastated, our bodies should process them. Be that as it may, our stomach related framework has less work to do with a smoothie than if we were to eat the fixings that way. Indeed, on the off chance that it doesn't sound that delightful, a few of the smoothie's stomach-related work was as of now done whereas blending.

The list of fixings for smoothies is exceptionally assorted. You'll put verdant greens, other vegetables, natural products, nuts, grains, superfoods, protein supplements, herbs, flavors, almost anything in a smoothie.

Q4. What is healthier? Freshly crushed juice is exceptionally sound. Particularly for people who have stomach related issues or are something else sick. Since juices don't contain fiber or mash, the body ought not to work with the liquid. They moreover cleanse the body. Usually furthermore due to the reality that there's no

- Digestion
- Absorption
- Assimilation

So, the body can primarily bargain with detoxification and the breaking down of other trash. Juices grant the body the opportunity to utilize its vitality to mend itself, whereas retaining supplements that are not found in plain water.

Smoothies, on the other hand, are like a little feast. So, on the off chance that you do not have time to sit down for a genuine dinner, you'll be able undoubtedly to utilize a smoothie as a substitute. They are remarkably suggested before or after work out since they don't contain any overwhelming eat less. So, you do not feel full and still have gotten imperative supplements that the body needs, especially after work out. Smoothies are a great choice after you have wrapped up a quick since they gradually get your body utilized to healthy nourishments. They also offer assistance cleanse the insides since they contain precisely the fiber that flushes the interiors through. Harms are bound and flushed out of our system. And if you need to begin coordinating more crude vegetables into your count calories, you'll do this exceptionally richly with smoothies.

Q5. How do you make smoothies and juices? To press a juice, you wish - of course, a juicer or a juicer. Qualification is made between juicers (electric or manual) and centrifuge juicers. In programmed centrifugal juicers, a sifter turns like a serving of mixed greens spinner, and the juice at that point runs through the strainer, which catches the mash. For speedy utilization, particularly when cooking, I inclined toward a manual citrus press that I still got to press myself. You'll clean them quicker after squeezing. Either within the dishwasher or fair flush with water.

Since I utilize the press exceptionally frequently amid the day, for example, for lemon juice, orange juice, and when cooking, usually exceptionally commonsense. The hand press does not work for verdant vegetables. For green juices, you would like an electrically operated juicer, which turns the vegetables (centrifuge juicer) or chops them (juicer) and, in this way, extricates the juice. Usually, exceptionally significant for the body since our bodies do not have the proteins to split the cell dividers in verdant vegetables.

You wish an electrically worked juicer for green juices, which turns the vegetables (centrifuge juicer) or chops them (juicer) and hence extricates the juice. Usually exceptionally significant for the body since our bodies don't have the chemicals to break the cell dividers in verdant vegetables.

So, after you make green juices, the body gets supplements that are bolted within the cells. Juicers with one or two screws can juice almost any natural product and vegetable, but too herbs and grasses. The screws to begin with break off pieces of the squeezed fabric and after that crush them out. The juice is isolated through a strainer, whereas the pomace (the filaments and mash) is launched after the twist drill. The speed of the snails is moo, which is why small oxygen gets into the juice.

Thus, the quality of the liquid is high.
For smoothies, I suggest a high-speed blender if you need to appreciate smoothies routinely within the future. It takes much longer to partition the pomace with a powerless or moderate blender (the strands and mash) from the juice. At that point, there's more oxygen within the smoothie, and numerous supplements oxidize with the oxygen.

This implies the smoothie contains fewer nutrients. That doesn't happen with an effective high-speed blender. Several plants are not exceptionally appropriate for smoothies because they are troublesome to blend. You'll discover out more approximately this here. In this video, you'll see the distinction again. Q6. Which fixings are not reasonable for juices and smoothies? You shouldn't utilize bland vegetables that are troublesome to process. For the case, sweet potatoes and typical potatoes contain a parcel of starch.

Root vegetables are too disturbing to process in smoothies. These fixings are problematic for the body to handle, indeed on the off chance, they have been blended. Superior to utilize water-rich vegetables and verdant greens.

Don't utilize as well numerous fixings! It is simple to delude you into using and numerous fixings since you think the more the superior. There are too multiple sound fixings, but you do not need to use them all at once in a smoothie. This will indeed have an inverse impact. 2-6 fixings are adequate. Smoothies and juices are as it were a portion of the diet. And you can't say one is way better than the other. Depending on when and in which circumstance you utilize them, they are the proper choice. As continuously, the assortment is the best. Q7. What else is there to consider? Not as well much fruit - It is superior for the body and particularly for the liver on the off chance that there are not as well numerous natural products within the juice or smoothie. Since as well, much fructose within the circulation system overpowers the liver. Of course, juices without natural products and as it were with vegetables are best. But of course, a small sweet taste isn't to be detested. I, as it was prescribed, including a few apples to it. You've got to choose for yourself.

Little spinach or Swiss chard: Spinach and Swiss chard contain oxalates and can cause kidney stones. I recommend only using spinach and Swiss chard now and then. To be sure. Otherwise, you can use any leafy vegetables every day.

COMMON MISTAKES TO AVOID IN MEDITERRANEAN RECIPES.

You should avoid these unhealthy foods and ingredients:

* Added sugar: Soda, candies, ice cream, table sugar and many others.

* Refined grains: White bread, pasta made with refined wheat, etc.

* Trans fats: Found in margarine and various processed foods.

* Refined oils: Soybean oil, canola oil, cottonseed oil and others.

* Processed meat: Processed sausages, hot dogs, etc.

* Highly processed foods: Anything labeled "low-fat" or "diet" or which looks like it was made in a factory.

How to Follow the Diet at Restaurants

It's very simple to make most restaurant meals suitable for the Mediterranean diet.

* Choose fish or seafood as your main dish.

* Ask them to fry your food in extra virgin olive oil.

* Only eat whole-grain bread, with olive oil instead of butter.

A Mediterranean Sample Menu for 1 Week

Below is a sample menu for one week on the Mediterranean diet.

Feel free to adjust the portions and food choices based on your own needs and preferences.

Monday

Breakfast: Greek yogurt with strawberries and oats.

Lunch: Whole-grain sandwich with vegetables.

Dinner: A tuna salad, dressed in olive oil. A piece of fruit for dessert.

Tuesday

Breakfast: Oatmeal with raisins.

Lunch: Leftover tuna salad from the night before.

Dinner: Salad with tomatoes, olives and feta cheese.

Wednesday

Breakfast: Omelet with veggies, tomatoes and onions. A piece of fruit.

Lunch: Whole-grain sandwich, with cheese and fresh vegetables.

Dinner: Mediterranean lasagne.

Thursday

Breakfast: Yogurt with sliced fruits and nuts.

Lunch: Leftover lasagne from the night before.

Dinner: Broiled salmon, served with brown rice and vegetables.

Friday

Breakfast: Eggs and vegetables, fried in olive oil.

Lunch: Greek yogurt with strawberries, oats and nuts.

Dinner: Grilled lamb, with salad and baked potato.

Saturday

Breakfast: Oatmeal with raisins, nuts and an apple.

Lunch: Whole-grain sandwich with vegetables.

Dinner: Mediterranean pizza made with whole wheat, topped with cheese, vegetables and olives.

Sunday

Breakfast: Omelet with veggies and olives.

Lunch: Leftover pizza from the night before.

Dinner: Grilled chicken, with vegetables and a potato. Fruit for dessert.

There is usually no need to count calories or track macronutrients (protein, fat and carbs) on the Mediterranean diet.

Table of Contents

#401. CAPRESE AVOCADO TOAST

Ready in about: 20 mins | serve: 2 | Nutritional value: Cal: 649g; Protein: 23.9g; Fat: 24.6g; Fiber: 10.5g; Carb: 86.4g

Ingredients

2 slices hearty sandwich bread, such as peasant bread, sourdough, whole-wheat or multi-grain

1 medium avocado, halved and pit removed

8 grape tomatoes, halved

2 ounces fresh ciliegine or bite-sized mozzarella balls (about 12)

4 large fresh basil leaves, torn

2 tbsp balsamic glaze

Instructions

Toasted the bread. While the bread is toasting, mash the avocado in a small bowl.

Spread the mashed avocado over the toast. Top each slice with tomatoes, mozzarella balls, and basil leaves, then drizzle with balsamic glaze. Serve immediately.

#402. CRISPY WHITE BEANS WITH GREENS AND POACHED EGG

Ready in about: 25 mins | serve: 4 | Nutritional value: Cal: 301g; Protein: 15.5g; Fat: 15.5g; Fiber: 6.4g; Carb: 26.5g

Ingredients

3 tbsp olive oil, divided

1 (15-ounce) can cannellini beans, drained and rinsed

1 tsp kosher salt, divided

2 tsp za'atar, divided

1 medium bunch Swiss chard (about 10 ounces), stems removed and leaves thinly sliced

2 cloves garlic, minced

1/4 tsp red pepper flakes, plus more for serving

1 tbsp freshly squeezed lemon juice

4 large eggs, poached

Instructions

Heat 2 tablespoons of the oil in a large frying pan over medium-high heat until shimmering. Add the beans, spread into an even layer, and cook undisturbed until the beans are lightly browned on the bottom, 2 to 4 minutes.

Add 1/2 teaspoon of the salt and 1 teaspoon of the za'atar, and stir to combine. Spread the beans out again and cook, stirring as needed, until golden-brown and blistered on all sides, 3 to 5 minutes more.

Add the remaining 1 tablespoon oil to the pan. Add the chard, remaining 1/2 teaspoon salt, remaining 1 teaspoon za'atar, garlic, and red pepper flakes. Cook, stirring occasionally, until the chard is wilted, 3 to 5 minutes. Remove the pan from the heat, add the lemon juice, and toss to combine.

Divide the beans and greens among 4 bowls, and top each with a poached egg and more red pepper flakes. Serve warm.

#403. EGGS WITH SUMMER TOMATOES, ZUCCHINI, AND BELL PEPPERS

Ready in about: 15 mins | serve: 2 | Nutritional value: Cal: 226g; Protein: 15.5g; Fat: 12.5g; Fiber: 6.3g; Carb: 20.6g

Ingredients

1 tbsp olive oil

1 small yellow onion, halved and thinly sliced

1 clove garlic, minced

2 medium summer squash or zucchini (approximately 4 cups)

2 medium tomatoes, chopped (approximately 3 cups)

1/2 tsp fresh thyme (optional)

1 tsp ground Spanish piquillo pepper or Spanish paprika

1 medium red bell pepper (see Recipe Note)

Salt and pepper

2 large eggs

Instructions

Heat the olive oil in a large, heavy skillet over medium heat. Add the onion and cook, stirring often, until translucent, about 5 minutes. Add the garlic and cook for another minute. Add squash and cook until it begins to soften and brown, about 10 minutes. Add the tomatoes, thyme (if using), and piquillo or paprika, and let simmer until everything is cooked down thick and stewy, about 20 minutes.

While the ratatouille is cooking, roast the pepper on the stovetop; see How To Roast Peppers on the Stovetop. Once it has cooled, remove the core and seeds, and cut into 1-inch pieces. Remove the skillet from the heat, add the roasted peppers, and salt and pepper to taste. Let the dish cool before serving — it's best served warm or at room temperature.

Fry the eggs (see how here), or prepare them however you prefer. Divide the vegetables between two plates, and top with the eggs. Serve with buttered toast.

#404. FLUFFY LEMON RICOTTA PANCAKES

Ready in about: 18 mins | serve: 4 | Nutritional value:
Cal: 344g; Protein: 17.7g; Fat: 15.9g; Fiber: 1.3g; Carb:
32.3g

Ingredients

4 large eggs

1 medium lemon

1 cup whole-milk ricotta cheese

1/2 cup whole or 2% milk

1 cup all-purpose flour

1 tbsp granulated sugar

1 tsp baking powder

1/4 tsp kosher salt

Unsalted butter, for cooking

For topping: citrus segments, fresh berries, lemon curd, or maple syrup

Instructions

Separate 4 large eggs, placing the whites in the bowl of stand mixer fitted with the whisk attachment and the yolks in a large bowl. (Alternatively, you can place the whites in a medium bowl if using an electric hand mixer or whisking by hand with a sturdy whisk.)

Finely grate the zest 1 medium lemon onto the egg yolks, then squeeze the juice from the lemon into the bowl (about 1 tablespoon zest and 3 tablespoons juice). Add 1 cup whole-milk ricotta cheese and 1/2 cup whole or 2% milk, and whisk to combine. Add 1 cup all-purpose flour, 1 tablespoon granulated sugar, 1 teaspoon baking powder, and 1/4 teaspoon kosher salt, and whisk until just combined; do not overmix.

Beat the egg whites on medium-high speed until stiff peaks form, 2 to 3 minutes. (Alternatively, beat with an electric hand mixer or sturdy whisk.) Stir 1/3 of the beaten egg whites into the egg yolk batter with a rubber spatula to lighten it. Then gently fold the remaining egg whites in until just combined; do not overmix.

Heat a large cast iron or nonstick skillet or griddle over medium heat. Add 1 teaspoon unsalted butter to the pan and swirl to coat. Drop the batter into the pan in 1/4 cup portions, 3 at a time. If needed, use the bottom of the measuring cup or the spatula to gently spread out each portion into rough 4-inch rounds. Cook until bubbles appear on the surface, the edges begin to look dry, and the bottoms are golden-brown, 2 to 3 minutes. Flip the pancakes and cook until the other side is golden-brown, 2 to 3 minutes more.

Transfer the pancakes to a warm oven or plate. Repeat cooking the remaining batter, using 1 teaspoon butter for each batch and wiping out the skillet between batches, as needed. Serve the pancakes immediately, with topping of choice.

#405. EASY SHEET PANS BAKED EGGS AND VEGGIES

Ready in about: 20 mins | serve: 6| Nutritional value:
Cal: 111g; Protein: 6.9g; Fat: 7.3g; Fiber: 1.6g; Carb:
4.9g

Description

Turn a few eggs and some veggies into the perfect meal!
These baked eggs with bell peppers and onions takes
one sheet pan and come together in 20 minutes! Easy.
Satisfying. And incredibly delicious. And you can
totally make this recipe your own to use up what
veggies you have on hand!

Ingredients

1 green bell pepper, cored and thinly sliced

1 orange bell pepper, cored and thinly sliced

1 red bell pepper, cored and thinly sliced

1 medium red onion, halved then thinly sliced

Salt and black pepper

Spices of your choice (I used 2 tsp za'atar blend, 1 tsp ground cumin and 1 tsp Aleppo chili pepper)

Extra virgin olive oil (I used Early Harvest Greek extra virgin olive oil)

6 large eggs

Chopped fresh parsley, a large handful

1 Roma tomato, diced

Crumbled feta, a small bit to your liking (optional)

Instructions

Preheat the oven to 400 degrees F.

Place sliced bell peppers (all colors) in a large mixing bowl. Add red onions. Season with kosher salt and pepper, 1 tsp za'atar, 1 tsp cumin and 1 tsp Aleppo chili pepper (keep the remaining za'atar for later). Drizzle with extra virgin olive oil. Toss to coat.

Transfer the pepper and onion medley to a large sheet pan. Spread in one layer. Bake in heated oven for 10 to 15 minutes.

Remove pan from oven briefly. Carefully make 6 "holes" or openings among the roasted veggies. Carefully crack each egg into a hole, keeping the yoke intact (it helps to crack the egg in a small dish to slide carefully into each hole.)

Return pan to oven and bake until the egg whites settle. Watch the yokes to see them turn to the doness you like (anywhere from 5 to 8 minutes).

Remove from oven. Season eggs to your liking. Sprinkle remaining 1 tsp za'atar all over. Add parsley, diced tomatoes, and a sprinkle of feta. Serve immediately!

#406. CRUSTLESS ZUCCHINI QUICHE RECIPE

Ready in about: 45 mins | serve: 8 | Nutritional value: Cal: 145g; Protein: 8.4g; Fat: 6.5g; Fiber: 0.6g; Carb: 16.8g

Ingredients

1 medium tomato sliced into thin rounds

Private Reserve extra virgin olive oil

1 zucchini, sliced into rounds (about 8 ounces sliced zucchini)

3 shallots, sliced into rounds (about 3.5 ounces sliced shallots)

Kosher salt and pepper

1 tsp sweet Spanish paprika, divided

½ cup part-skim shredded mozzarella (nearly 2 ounces)

2 tbsp grated Parmesan (about 0.35 ounces)

3 large eggs, beaten

⅔ cup skim milk

¼ tsp baking powder

½ cup white whole wheat flour OR all-purpose flour (about 2 ounces), sifted

¼ cup packed fresh parsley (about 0.2 ounces)

Instructions

Preheat the oven to 350 degrees F.

Arrange sliced tomatoes on paper towel and sprinkle with salt. Leave for a few minutes, then pat dry.

Meanwhile, in a large cooking skillet, heat 2 tbsp Private Reserve extra virgin olive oil over medium heat until shimmering but not smoking. Add zucchini and shallots. Season with kosher salt, pepper, and ½ tsp sweet paprika. Raise heat slightly, and Sautee, tossing regularly, until vegetables are tender and nicely colored (with some brown spots on zucchini).

Transfer the cooked zucchini and shallots mixture to the bottom of a lightly oiled 9-inch pie dish like this one. Arrange sliced tomatoes on top. Add mozzarella, and Parmesan (spread evenly across).

In a mixing bowl, whisk together eggs, milk, remaining ½ tsp paprika, baking powder, flour, and fresh parsley.

Pour egg mixture into the pie dish on top of the cheese mixture.

Bake in 350 degrees F heated-oven for about 30 minutes or until the egg mixture is well set in the dish. Remove from oven and wait 5 to 7 minutes before slicing to serve (Quiche will puff up slightly because of the baking powder, but will quickly go down as it sits.)

#407. EASY FIG PASTRY RECIPE

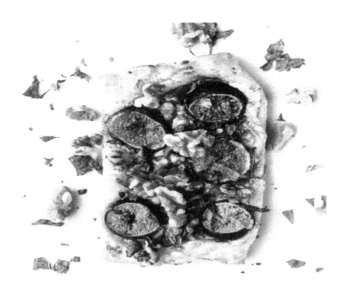

Ready in about: 35 mins | serve: 4 | Nutritional value:
Cal: 703g; Protein: 14.1g; Fat: 51.5g; Fiber: 20.3g;
Carb: 47.6g

Ingredients

1 sheet of good store-bought puff pastry, thawed in
fridge for 3 hours or so
8 oz fresh black mission figs
4-5 oz goat cheese, room temperature
¼ cup walnuts, roughly chopped; more for garnish if
desired
2 tbsp good fig jam
1 tbsp butter, melted
¼ cup fresh mint leaves, roughly chopped (optional)

Instructions

Preheat oven to 375F.

Divide thawed puff pastry into four fairly equal rectangular pieces and place on baking sheet lined with parchment paper.

Spread goat cheese on each piece. Add jam, figs and then chopped walnuts.

Brush figs and edges of puff pastry with melted butter. Slightly turn pastry edges up.

Bake in 375F oven for 18-20 minutes or until pastry is golden and puffy.

Garnish with chopped mint leaves and more walnuts, if desired.

Check out our other flaky recipes like phyllo pizza or phyllo meat pie. Craving sweeter and nuttier? See our Greek yogurt parfait with Kahlua and nuts.

#408. EASY BREAKFAST STUFFED PEPPERS

Ready in about: 20 mins | serve: 6 | Nutritional value: Cal: 107g; Protein: 20.5g; Fat: 22.5g; Fiber: 0.6g; Carb: 7.4g

Ingredients

3 bell peppers, any color, halved length-wise and cored water

Private Reserve Greek extra virgin olive oil

6 oz mushrooms, any kind, sliced or chopped

1 cup chopped yellow onion

1o to 12 oz gold potatoes, peeled and diced small

Salt and pepper

¾ tsp all-natural Aleppo pepper

¾ tsp organic coriander

¾ tsp organic cumin

½ tsp organic turmeric

3 garlic cloves, chopped

½ cup chopped or sliced cherry tomatoes

½ cup packed chopped fresh parsley

6 eggs

Instructions

Preheat oven to 350 degrees F.

Arrange pepper halves in a baking dish or cast-iron skillet. Add 1 cup water to the bottom of dish or skillet. Cover with foil and bake in heated oven for 10 to 15 minutes.

Meanwhile, make the potato hash stuffing. Begin by heating a 12-inch cast iron skillet over high heat. Add mushrooms, cook tossing regularly until nicely browned. Season with salt. Remove from skillet.

Turn heat to medium-high. To the skillet, add 2 tbsp extra virgin olive oil. When oil is shimmering but not smoking (which will be quick), add onions and potatoes. Season with salt and pepper and the spices. Cook, stirring regularly for 5 minutes. Add the garlic, and continue to cook over medium-high heat, stirring regularly, until potatoes are tender, another 5 to 7 minutes or so.

Now, add the cooked mushrooms, tomato, and parsley to the potatoes. Stir to combine. Remove from heat.

Remove pepper halves from oven (do not drain water.) Stuff each with the potato stuffing about ¾ of the way. Now, carefully crack one egg into each pepper over the potato stuffing.

Cover with aluminum foil (make sure to tent the foil so it does not stick to the egg yolks.) Bake in heated oven for 18 to 20 minutes, or until the eggs are soft set (longer if you like the eggs more cooked.) Serve immediately!

#409. EASY GREEK EASTER BREAD RECIPE

Ready in about: 4 hours 45 minutes| serve: 1 large loaf (16 slices) | Nutritional value: Cal: 252g; Protein: 7.3g; Fat: 6.6g; Fiber: 5.6g; Carb: 40.6g

Ingredients

2 ¼ tsp active dry yeast (1 envelope)

5 ½ cups all-purpose flour, more for dusting

½ cup sugar

1 ⅓ cup milk

5 tbsp unsalted butter

1 tsp fine salt

2 large eggs, beaten, PLUS 1 egg beaten with 1 tsp water (egg wash)

2 tbsp anise seed

¼ tsp vanilla extract

3 hard-boiled eggs, dyed red and fully dried

Olive oil

2 to 4 tbsp toasted sesame seeds (optional)

Instructions

In the bowl of a stand mixer, combine ⅓ cup hot water (about 110 degrees F) with the yeast, 1 tbsp of the flour, and 1 tbsp of the sugar. Whisk gently. Cover with a towel and leave aside for 10 minutes until bubbly.

In the meantime, heat the milk in a small sauce pan until the edges begin to bubble, about 4 to 6 minutes. Remove from heat and stir in the butter, remaining sugar and salt. Set aside for 5 minutes to cool.

Using the paddle attachment of your stand mixer, stir the milk mixture into the yeast mixture. While paddle is stirring, add the 2 beaten eggs. Gradually mix in the flour, anise seed, and vanilla extract. Beat unit a soft dough forms. Increase speed to medium (or medium-high if needed) until the dough pulls away from the sides of the bowl.

Transfer dough onto a lightly floured surface (dough will be sticky at this point.) Kneed by hand until very smooth (about 5 minutes), then place dough into a lightly-oiled bowl. Cover and place in a warm, closed space for 1 ½ hours, until doubled in size. (I had heated my oven to lowest temperature, then turned it off a few minutes before placing my covered dough in.)

Punch dough down, and transfer to floured surface again. Cut dough into 3 equal parts, and gently roll each to form a long 16-inch rope. Transfer to a large baking sheet lined with parchment paper. Press ropes together at one end and braid fairly loosely. Form into a circle and press together on the other side. Stretch the circle to about 10 inches across and the hole in the middle about 3 ½ inches wide.

Cover with a clean towel and place back in warm space for 1 hour until doubled in size.

Rub the dyed eggs with olive oil, and buff with paper towel. Select three spots in the dough, evenly spaced, and gently insert the eggs. Cover and return to warm space. Let rise 1 more hour until dough doubles in size.

Heat oven to 350 degrees F. Brush the bread with the egg wash and sprinkle with toasted sesame seeds. Bake about 45 minutes until braided loaf turns a nice deep golden brown (should sound hallow when you tap on it.)

Let cool for about 30 minutes before serving. Serve with more boiled eggs, honey or other breakfast items. Enjoy!

#410. GREEN SHAKSHUKA RECIPE

Ready in about: 30 mins | serve: 4 | Nutritional value: Cal: 229.6g; Protein: 9g; Fat: 18.2g; Fiber: 3g;Carb: 6.4g

Ingredients

¼ cup extra virgin olive oil, more for later
8 ounces brussels sprouts. trimmed and thinly sliced

Kosher salt
½ large red onion, finely chopped
3 garlic cloves, minced
1 large bunch kale (8 ounces), thick veins and stems removed, chopped
2 cups baby spinach (about 2.5 ounces),
1 tsp Aleppo pepper (or ½ tsp crushed red pepper flakes)
1 tsp coriander
¾ tsp cumin
Juice of ½ lemons
4 large eggs
1 green onion, trimmed and chopped, both white and green parts
Handful fresh parsley for garnish
Crumbled feta for garnish

Instructions

In a 10-inch pan or skillet with a lid, heat the extra virgin olive oil over medium-high heat until shimmering but not smoking. Add the sliced brussels sprouts and sprinkle with a dash of kosher salt. Cook for about 5 to 6 minutes, tossing occasionally until they soften and gain some color (I like a little bit of char).

Reduce the heat to medium. Add the onions and garlic, and cook, tossing regularly for 3 to 4 minutes until softened (don't let the garlic burn though, manage the heat as you need to).

Add the kale and toss for 5 minutes until it wilts a little (you may have to add it to the pan in stages). Add the spinach and toss to combine. Season with a pinch of kosher salt.

Add the spices and toss to combine. Add ½ cup of water. Turn the heat to medium-low. Cover and let cook for about 8 to 10 minutes until the kale has completely wilted. Stir in the lemon juice.

Using a spoon, make 4 wells. Crack an egg into each well and season each egg with a bit of salt. Cover the pan and cook for another 4 minutes or until the eggs have settled to your liking (I like a runny yoke). Remove from the heat. Add another drizzle of extra virgin olive oil if you like. Garnish with the fresh green onions, parsley and some creamy feta. Serve immediately with your favorite bread or warm pita.

#411. HEARTY BREAKFAST FRUIT SALAD

Ready in about: 20 mins | serve: 5 | Nutritional value: Cal: 282g; Protein: 3.7g; Fat: 16.0g; Fiber: 6.6g; Carb: 34.8g

Ingredients

For the grains:

1 cup pearl or hulled barley or any sturdy whole grain (see the list above)

3 cups water

3 tbsp olive or vegetable oil, divided

1/2 tsp kosher salt

For the fruit (see list above):

1/2 large pineapple, peeled and cut into 1 1/2- to 2-inch chunks (2 to 2 1/2 cups)

6 medium tangerines or mandarins, or 5 large oranges (about 1 1/2 pounds total)

1 1/4 cups pomegranate seeds

1 small bunch fresh mint

For the dressing:

1/3 cup honey or another sweetener (see list above)

Juice and finely grated zest of 1 lemon (about 1/4 cup juice)

Juice and finely grated zest of 2 limes (about 1/4 cup juice)

1/2 tsp kosher salt

1/4 cup olive oil

1/4 cup toasted hazelnut or nut oil

Equipment

2 Soft silicone spatula

2 saucepans or 1 saucepan and a microwave-safe bowl

Sharp knife

3 large airtight containers with covers

2 smaller airtight containers with covers

1 (3-cup) airtight container with a cover

Mixing bowl

Wire whisk

Instructions

Rinse the grain: Line 2 rimmed baking sheets with parchment paper. Rinse the barley in a strainer under cold water until the water below is clear, about 1 minute. Gently shake the strainer to drain off any excess water. Place the barley on one of the prepared baking sheets and use a spatula to spread out the grains into a single layer. Let dry completely, 3 to 5 minutes.

Heat the water: Warm the water on the stovetop or in the microwave; set aside.

Toast the grain: Heat 2 tablespoons of the oil in a medium saucepan over high heat until shimmering. Carefully add the barley and toast, stirring constantly, until they just begin to darken a bit, 1 minute to 90 seconds.

Add the water: Add the warm water and salt and bring to a boil. Reduce the heat to a simmer or the lowest setting your stovetop has, cover, and cook until tender and most of the liquid has been absorbed, 40 to 45 minutes. Remove the pot from the heat and let stand, covered, for 10 minutes, to let the barley steam and finish absorbing the water. Meanwhile, prep the fruit, mint, and dressing.

Prepare the fruit: Place the pineapple chunks into one of the large containers. Peel and cut the tangerines, mandarins, or oranges into segments, removing as much of the bitter white pith as you can. Place in another container, cover, and refrigerate. Refrigerate the pomegranate seeds separately in a covered container.

Prepare the mint: Thinly slice or mince the mint leaves. Refrigerate in its own covered container.

Make the dressing: Whisk the honey, juice and zests, and salt together in a medium bowl. Drizzle in the olive oil, then the nut oil, while whisking constantly until incorporated. Cover and refrigerate, or refrigerate in a jar.

Dry and cool the grain: Transfer the cooked barley onto the second prepared baking sheet and spread into an even layer. Let cool completely, 10 to 20 minutes. Drizzle the barley with the remaining 1 tablespoon of oil and mix to coat.

Chill the cooked grain: Transfer the barley to a large container, cover, and refrigerate.

Assemble the salad and eat: To serve, scoop 2/3 cup of the barley into each bowl. Add about 6 pieces of pineapple, 10 to 12 orange segments, and 1/4 cup pomegranate seeds into each bowl. Add 1 to 2 tablespoons of the mint and 2 to 3 tablespoons of the dressing to each bowl (re-whisk the dressing if needed). Stir to mix and coat with the dressing.

#412. HEALTHY CARROT CAKE RECIPE WITH HONEY AND WHOLE WHEAT FLOUR

Ready in about: 60 mins | serve: 12 | Nutritional value:
Cal: 168g; Protein: 5g; Fat: 8.6g; Fiber: 2.6g; Carb:
20.3g

Ingredients

½ cup Private Reserve Greek extra virgin olive oil

½ cup Greek yogurt (reduced fat)

⅓ cup milk (2% reduced fat milk)

½ cup quality dark honey

3 eggs at room temperature

2 ¼ cup whole wheat flour

1 ½ tsp baking powder

½ tsp salt

4 tsp ground cinnamon

½ tsp ground cardamom

¼ tsp ground ginger

2 cups finely grated carrots (you can use food processor
to very finely chop instead)

6 Medjool dates, pitted and finely chopped (you can use
food processor)

⅓ cup chopped walnuts

powdered sugar for light dusting

Instructions

Preheat oven to 350 degrees F.

In a large bowl, whisk the olive oil, geek yogurt, and milk. Add eggs one-by-one and whisk to combine.

In a separate bowl, whisk flour, baking powder, salt, and spices

Gradually add the dry ingredients to the wet ingredients, mixing with a wooden spoon.

Fold in the carrots. Mix to combine, then add the dates and walnuts. Again, mix with your wooden spoon until well combined.

Line a 9-inch square baking pan like this one with parchment paper (or coat well with olive oil). Pour the carrot cake batter into the pan.

Bake in 350 degrees F heated-oven for 1 hour (until a tooth pick inserted in middle of the cake comes out clean). Let cool completely. Sprinkle powdered sugar, if desired. Cut into 9 or 12 square pieces. Enjoy!

#413. KALE AND GOAT CHEESE FRITTATA CUPS

Ready in about: 20 mins | serve: 8 | Nutritional value:
Cal: 179g; Protein: 10.0g; Fat: 14.7g; Fiber: 0.3g; Carb:
1.2g

Ingredients

2 cups chopped lacinato kale

1 garlic clove, thinly sliced

3 tbsp olive oil

1/4 tsp red pepper flakes

8 large eggs

1/4 tsp salt

Dash ground black pepper

1/2 tsp dried thyme

1/4 cup goat cheese, crumbled

Instructions

Preheat the oven to 350°F. To get 2 cups kale, remove the leaves from the kale ribs. Wash and dry the leaves and cut them into 1/2-inch-wide strips.

In a 10-inch nonstick skillet, cook the garlic in 1 tablespoon of oil over medium-high heat for 30 seconds. Add the kale and red pepper flakes and cook until wilted, 1 to 2 minutes.

In a medium bowl, beat the eggs with the salt and pepper. Add the kale and thyme to the egg mixture.

Using a 12-cup muffin tin, use the remaining 2 tablespoons of oil to grease 8 of the cups (you may also use butter or nonstick spray if you'd prefer). Sprinkle the tops with goat cheese. Bake until they are set in the center, about 25 to 30 minutes.

Frittata is best eaten warm from the oven or within the next day, but leftovers can be kept refrigerated and reheated for up to a week.

#414. KUKU SABZI: BAKED PERSIAN HERB
     OMELET

Ready in about: 40 mins | serve: 6 | Nutritional value: Cal: 184g; Protein:7.1g; Fat: 16.7g

Ingredients

4 ½ cup all-purpose flour or white bread flour

2 tbsp sugar

2 tsp salt

1 ½ cups whole milk (or unsweetened almond milk for vegan option) warm

1 tbsp active dry yeast fast-action

1 tsp baking powder

Olive oil

For the sesame coating

1 cup sesame seeds I used raw white sesame seeds

1 to 2 tbsp honey

INSTRUCTIONS

Mix and knead the dough. Put the flour, sugar, salt, milk, yeast, and baking powder in the bowl of a freestanding mixer fitted with the dough hook (do not add the olive oil yet). Mix on medium speed until the dough comes together forming a soft and pliable ball. If you do not have a mixer, mix the dough ingredients in a large bowl and knead by hand (you can knead on a clean surface if that is easier for you) until the dough is smooth and pliable (it will take a bit longer this way, but will work). You are looking for a soft, elastic but robust dough.

Allow the dough to rise. Rub the dough with a little bit olive oil and place it in a large bowl. Cove with plastic wrap or a damp kitchen towel. Set aside in a warm spot for 1 hour; the dough should rise and double in size.

Work on the sesame coating. In a large shallow baking dish, combine the sesame seeds and honey with 1 tablespoon of water. Mix, adding a bit more water as necessary, until you have a wet mixture that is neither too sticky and thick that it clumps up, nor too thin (you'll need to be able to coat the dough in the sesame seeds and have them stick).

Divide the dough and make 6 equal pieces. Punch down the risen dough and divide it into 6 portions that are equal in size. Place them on a lightly floured work surface. Roll and stretch each piece into a log (about 8-12 inches long), then attach the ends together to form a ring (you should end up with 6 rings). Gently stretch out the rings to form ovals rather than circles. Set aside for 15 minutes to rest.

Heat the oven to 450 degrees F (gas mark 8).

Coat the rings or bagels with the sesame coating. Take each dough ring and dip it in the sesame mixture. Set it on a large baking sheet. Repeat with the remaining rings. Allow the rings to rest on the baking sheet one more time for 10 minutes.

Bake. Place the baking sheet (or sheets) in the heated oven and bake for 15 to 20 minutes or until the bagels cook through and turn a deep golden color

#416. JERUSALEM BAGEL RECIPE

Ready in about: 1 hr 20 mins | serve: 6 | Nutritional value: Cal: 396.5g; Protein: 11.9g; Fat: 3g; Fiber: 2.7g; Carb: 78.9g
Fiber: 2.6g; Carb: 3.1g

Ingredients

5 tbsp Private Reserve Greek extra virgin olive oil

2 cups flat-leaf parsley, leaves

2 cups cilantro, leaves and tender stems

1 cup roughly chopped fresh dill

6 scallions, trimmed and coarsely chopped

1 ½ tsp baking powder

1 tsp kosher salt

¾ tsp ground green cardamom

¾ tsp ground cinnamon

½ tsp ground cumin

¼ tsp ground black pepper

6 large eggs

½ cup walnuts, toasted and chopped (optional)

⅓ cup dried cranberries, coarsely chopped (optional)

Instructions

Position an oven rack in the upper-middle position and heat oven to 375 degrees F.

Trace the bottom of an 8-inch square pan or 9-inch round cake pan on kitchen parchment, then cut inside the lines to create a piece to fit in the bottom of the pan.

Coat the bottom and sides of the pan with 2 tbsp extra virgin olive oil, turning the parchment to coat on both sides (the oil should pool at the bottom and generously coat the sides).

In a food processor, combine the parsley, cilantro, dill, scallions and the remaining 3 tbsp extra virgin olive oil. Process until finely ground (now, I like my herbs less fine, so I stopped the processor at my desired texture). Set aside for now.

In a large bowl, whisk the baking powder, salt, cardamom, cinnamon, cumin and pepper. Add 2 eggs and whisk until blended, then add the remaining eggs and whisk until just combined. Fold in the herb-scallion mixture and the walnuts and cranberries, if using. Pour into the prepared pan and smooth the top.

Bake in 375 degrees F heated-oven until the center of the egg is firm, about 20 to 25 minutes. (The egg mixture will rise, but will go down once you set it aside to cool.)

Let the kuku cool in the pan undisturbed for 10 minutes. When ready, run a thin knife around the edges to loosen the kuku. Invert onto a plate and remove the parchment from bottom, then re-invert on another serving plate or a cutting board so the top of the kuku is facing you. Slice into wedges and serve warm or at room temperature.

Serve with a dollop of yogurt. See more suggestions in the post under "what to serve with kuku sabzi."

#417. MIDDLE EASTERN ZUCCHINI BAKED OMELET

Ready in about: 30 mins | serve: 6 | Nutritional value: Cal: 216g; Protein: 17.9g; Fat: 5.9g; Fiber: 4.3g; Carb: 6.4g

Ingredients

2 zucchinis, thinly sliced into rounds Salt

2 tbsp olive oil, more if needed

1 small onion, thinly sliced

½ tsp garlic powder

Whole bunch fresh mint, stems removed (about 30 mint leaves), torn

8 large eggs

pinch red pepper flakes, to your taste

½ tsp baking powder

2 slices of bread (toast), crust removed and soaked in ⅓ cup milk

Feta cheese for garnish (optional)

Lemon juice to serve

Sliced tomatoes to serve (optional)

Instructions

Preheat the oven to 350 degrees F.

Sprinkle the zucchini slices with a little salt and set aside for 15 minutes. Pat the zucchini dry.

In a 10-inch cast iron skillet (or oven safe skillet), heat the olive oil on medium, then add the zucchini and onions. Raise the heat to medium-high and saute the vegetables for 5-7 minutes or until they are tender and golden in color. Add most of the torn mint leaves; set aside some for later. Turn the heat off and let cool.

In a medium mixing bowl, whisk the eggs, salt, crushed red pepper, and the baking powder. Squeeze the toast to drain any excess milk, then break it apart with your hands and add the bread pieces to the eggs. Whisk again briefly.

Now stir the zucchini and onions in the egg mixture. If needed, add a little more olive oil to the cast iron skillet. Transfer the egg mixture to the skillet.

Bake in the 350 F degrees heated oven for 15-20 minutes, or until the surface of the omelet looks done.

Top the zucchini baked omelet with feta cheese if you like. And garnish with the torn mint leaves you set aside earlier. Serve with lemon wedges on the side and sliced fresh vegetables like tomatoes. A great side dish to this zucchini baked omelet is fattoush salad.

#418. MEDITERRANEAN BREAKFAST PITAS

Ready in about: 20 mins | serve: 4 | Nutritional value: Cal: 206g; Protein: 12.0g; Fat: 8.3g; Fiber: 5.9g; Carb: 22.9g

Ingredients

4 large eggs, at room temperature

Salt

2 whole-wheat pita breads with pockets, cut in half

1/2 cup hummus (4 ounces)

1 medium cucumber, thinly sliced into rounds

2 medium tomatoes, large dice

Handful of fresh parsley leaves, coarsely chopped

Freshly ground black pepper

Hot sauce (optional)

Instructions

Fill a medium saucepan with water and bring to a boil. Gently place your room-temperature eggs in the water and cook for 7 minutes. Drain the water and run the eggs under cold water to cool. Peel the eggs and cut into 1/4-inch-thick slices. Sprinkle with salt and set aside.

Spread the inside of each pita pocket with 2 tablespoons of hummus. Place a few cucumber slices and some diced tomato into each pita. Sprinkle with salt and pepper. Tuck 1 sliced egg into each pita and sprinkle with parsley and hot sauce (if using).

#419. MEDITERRANEAN BREAKFAST EGG MUFFINS

Ready in about: 40 mins | serve: 12 | Nutritional value: Cal: 67g; Protein: 4.6g; Fat: 4.7g; Fiber: 5.1g; Carb: 5.2g

Ingredients

Extra virgin olive oil for brushing

1 small red bell pepper, chopped (about ¾ cup)

12 cherry tomatoes, halved

1 shallot, finely chopped

6 to 10 pitted kalamata olives, chopped

3 to 4 oz/113 g cooked chicken or turkey, boneless, shredded

1 oz/ 28. 34 g (about ½ cup) chopped fresh parsley leaves

Handful crumbled feta to your liking

8 large eggs

Salt and Pepper

½ tsp Spanish paprika

¼ tsp ground turmeric (optional)

Instructions

Place a rack in the center of your oven and preheat to 350 degrees F.

Prepare a 12-cup muffin pan like this one (or 12 individual muffin cups). Brush with extra virgin olive oil.

Divide the peppers, tomatoes, shallots, olives, chicken (or turkey), parsley, and crumbled feta among the 12 cups (they should come up to about ⅔ of the way full.)

In a large measuring cup or a mixing bowl, add eggs, salt, pepper, and spices. Whisk well to combine.

Pour the egg mixture carefully over each cup, leaving a little room at the top (should be about ¾ of the way or so.)

Place muffin pan or muffin cups on top of a sheet pan (to help catch any spills). Bake in heated oven for about 25 minutes or until the egg muffins are set.

Let cool for a few minutes, then run a small butter knife around the edges of each muffin to loosen. Remove from pan and serve!

#420. MEDITERRANEAN-STYLE BREAKFAST TOAST

Ready in about: 10 mins | serve: 4 | Nutritional value: Cal: 166g; Protein: 6.1g; Fat: 4.2g; Fiber: 6.0g; Carb: 29.4g

Ingredients

4 thick slices whole grain or whole wheat bread of choice

½ cup/123 g hummus (homemade or quality store-bought)

Za'atar spice blend, to your liking

Handful baby arugula

1 cucumber, sliced into rounds

1 to 2 Roma tomatoes, sliced into rounds

2 tbsp/about 16 g chopped olives of your choice

Crumbled feta cheese, a sprinkle to your liking

Instructions

Toast bread slices to your liking

Spread about 2 tbsp hummus on each slice of bread. Add a generous sprinkle of Za'atar spice, then load on the arugula and remaining toppings. Enjoy!

#421. MEDITERRANEAN BREAKFAST BOARD

Ready in about: 30 mins | serve: 6 | Nutritional value:
Cal: 437g; Protein: 23.5g; Fat: 35.5g; Fiber: 0.6g; Carb:
7.4g

Ingredients

1 Falafel Recipe

1 Classic Hummus Recipe (or roasted garlic hummus,
roasted red pepper hummus)

1 Baba Ganoush Recipe

Feta cheese or 1 Labneh Recipe

1 Tabouli Recipe

1 to 2 tomatoes, sliced

1 English cucumber, sliced

6 to 7 Radish, halved or sliced

Assorted olives (I like a mix of green olives and kalamata olives)

Marinated artichokes or mushrooms

Early Harvest EVOO and Za'atar to dip

Pita Bread, sliced into quarters

Grapes (palette cleanser)

Fresh herbs for garnish

Instructions

Make the falafel according to this recipe. You will need to begin at least the night before to soak the chickpeas. See notes below for working ahead. (You may also buy falafel at a local Middle Eastern store.)

Make the hummus according to this recipe, and Baba ganoush according to this recipe. You can prepare both of these the night before and store in the fridge. If you like, try roasted garlic hummus or roasted red pepper hummus to change things up. (If you don't have the time, use quality store-bought hummus.)

Slice feta cheese, or prepare Labneh ahead of time according to this recipe.

Make tabouli according to this recipe. Can be made a couple days in advance and refrigerated in tight-lid glass containers.

To assemble the Mediterranean breakfast board, place the hummus, baba ganoush, olive oil, za'atar, tabouli in bowls. Place the largest bowl in the center of a large wooden board or platter to create a focal point. Arrange the remaining bowls on different parts of the board or platter to create movement and shape. Use the gaps between the bowls to place the remaining ingredients like falafel, sliced vegetables, and pita bread. Add grapes and garnish with fresh herbs, if you like.

#422. MUESLI

Ready in about: 15 mins | serve: 8| Nutritional value: Cal: 275g; Protein: 8.5g; Fat: 13.0g; Fiber: 7.5g; Carb: 36.4g

Ingredients

3 1/2 cups rolled oats

1/2 cup wheat bran

1/2 tsp kosher salt

1/2 tsp ground cinnamon

1/2 cup sliced almonds

1/4 cup raw pecans, coarsely chopped

1/4 cup raw pepitas (shelled pumpkin seeds)

1/2 cup unsweetened coconut flakes

1/4 cup dried apricots, coarsely chopped

1/4 cup dried cherries

Equipment

Large rimmed baking sheet

Large airtight container, for storing

Instructions

Toast the grains, nuts, and seeds. Arrange 2 racks to divide the oven into thirds and heat to 350°F. Place the oats, wheat bran, salt, and cinnamon on a rimmed baking sheet; toss to combine; and spread into an even layer. Place the almonds, pecans, and pepitas on a second rimmed baking sheet; toss to combine; and spread into an even layer. Transfer both baking sheets to oven, placing oats on top rack and nuts on bottom. Bake until nuts are fragrant, 10 to 12 minutes.

Add the coconut. Remove the baking sheet with the nuts and set aside to cool. Sprinkle the coconut over the oats, return to the upper rack, and bake until the coconut is golden-brown, about 5 minutes more. Remove from oven and set aside to cool, about 10 minutes.

Transfer to a large bowl. Transfer the contents of both baking sheets to a large bowl.

Add the dried fruit. Add the apricots and cherries and toss to combine.

Transfer to an airtight container. Muesli can be stored in an airtight container at room temperature for up to 1 month.

Enjoy as desired. Enjoy as oatmeal, cereal, overnight oats, or with yogurt, topped with fresh fruit and a drizzle of honey or maple syrup, if desired.

#423. MEDITERRANEAN POTATO HASH WITH ASPARAGUS, CHICKPEAS AND POACHED EGGS

Ready in about: 24 mins | serve: 4 | Nutritional value: Cal: 535g; Protein: 26.6g; Fat: 20.8g; Fiber: 20.3g; Carb: 134.5g

Ingredients
Private Reserve extra virgin olive oil
1 small yellow onion, chopped
2 garlic cloves, chopped
2 russet potatoes, diced
Salt and pepper
1 cup canned chickpeas, drained and rinsed
1 lb baby asparagus, hard ends removed, chopped into ¼ inch pieces
1 ½ tsp ground allspice
1 tsp Za'atar
1 tsp dried oregano
1 tsp sweet paprika or smoked paprika

1 tsp coriander
Pinch sugar
4 eggs (to be poached)

Water
1 tsp White Vinegar
1 small red onion, finely chopped
2 Roma tomatoes, chopped
½ cup crumbled feta
1 cup chopped fresh parsley; stems removed

Instructions
Heat 1 ½ tbsp olive oil in a large cast-iron skillet. Turn the heat to medium-high and add the chopped onions, garlic and potatoes. Season with salt and pepper. Cook for 5-7 minutes, stirring frequently until the potatoes are tender (some of the potatoes may gain a bit of a golden crust, which is good!)

Add the chickpeas, asparagus, a dash more salt and pepper and the spices. Stir to combine. Cook for another 5-7 minutes. Turn the heat to low to keep the potato hash warm; stir regularly.

Meanwhile, bring a medium pot of water to a steady simmer and add 1 tsp vinegar. Break the eggs into a bowl. Stir the simmering water gently and carefully slide the eggs in. The egg whites should warp around the yoke. Cook for 3 minutes exactly, then remove the eggs from the simmering water and onto kitchen towel to drain briefly. Season with salt and pepper.

Remove the potato hash from the heat and add the chopped red onions, tomatoes, feta and parsley. Top with the poached eggs. Enjoy!

#424. LOADED MEDITERRANEAN OMELET

Ready in about: 2 mins | serve: 2 | Nutritional value: Cal: 168g; Protein: 23.5g; Fat: 10.7g; Fiber: 3.6g; Carb: 4g

Ingredients

4 large eggs

2 tbsp fat-free milk

¼ tsp baking powder (optional)

½ tsp Spanish paprika

¼ tsp ground allspice

Salt and pepper, to your liking (I used about ½ tsp each)

1 ½ tsp Private Reserve Greek extra virgin olive oil

1 tzatziki sauce recipe to serve, optional

Warm pita to serve, optional

Topping

½ cup cherry tomatoes, halved

2 tbsp sliced pitted Kalamata olives

¼ to ⅓ cup marinated artichoke hearts, drained and quartered

2 tbsp chopped fresh parsley, more for later

2 tbsp chopped fresh mint, more for later

Crumbled feta cheese, to your liking, optional

Instructions

In a mixing bowl, add the eggs, milk, baking powder (if using), spices, salt and pepper. Quickly and vigorously whisk to combine.

In a 10-inch non-stick skillet, heat extra virgin olive oil until shimmering but not smoking. Be sure to tilt the skillet to coat the bottom well with oil.

Pour the egg mixture in and immediately stir with a heat-resistant spatula for like 5 seconds. Then push the cooked portions at the edge toward the center, tilting the pan to allow uncooked egg to fill in around the edges. When no more egg runs to the sides, continue to cook until almost set and the bottom is light golden (about 1 minute.) Remember, the omelet has more time to cook once filled and folded.

Remove the skillet from the heat. Spoon a good portion of the toppings onto the center third of the omelet. Use the spatula to fold. Add the remainder of the toppings on top. Sprinkle a little fresher herb.

Slice the omelette into two halves and serve hot. If you like, add a side of Greek tzatziki sauce and warm pita bread. Enjoy!

#425. OPEN-FACED GREEK OMELET RECIPE WITH TOMATOES

Ready in about: 20 mins | serve: 4 | Nutritional value: Cal: 179g; Protein: 11.8g; Fat: 13g; Fiber: 0.2g; Carb: 3.7g

Ingredients

Quality Extra Virgin Olive Oil like this Private Reserve EVOO

1 large tomato, thickly sliced (4 slices)

1 garlic clove, minced

2 tbsp crumbled Greek feta cheese

7 large eggs

1 tbsp chopped fresh mint leaves

½ tsp baking powder

½ tsp sweet paprika

½ tsp dill weed

½ tsp coriander

Salt and black pepper

Instructions

In a non-stick, oven-safe pan like this one, heat 2 tbsp Private Reserve extra virgin olive oil over medium heat.

Add tomato slices, spread them in one even layer. Sprinkle minced garlic on top. Cook over medium heat, undisturbed, until tomatoes are soft and slightly dry (about 5 minutes). Add feta cheese and let melt a little.

While the tomatoes are frying, break the eggs into a large mixing bowl. Add baking powder, fresh mint, spices, salt and pepper. Whisk.

Turn up the heat to medium-high. Pour the egg mixture on top of the tomatoes. Cover loosely until the top begins to set.

Turn your oven broiler on. Transfer the egg skillet to oven. Broil briefly, watching carefully, until fully cooked.

Slice the Greek omelet into 4 pieces. Serve hot with your favorite bread and a side of Greek olives, or add a simple salad like this Mediterranean 3-bean salad or even Fattoush.

#426. OVERNIGHT BAKED FRENCH TOAST WITH CHALLAH

Ready in about: 45 mins | serve: 6 | Nutritional value: Cal: 452g; Protein: 18.8g; Fat: 10.7g; Fiber: 6.3g; Carb: 82.1g

Ingredients

6-8 challah bread slices, ¾-inch thick

2 tbsp soft unsalted butter, plus 1 tbsp cold unsalted butter

1 cup plain reduced-fat yogurt (not Greek yogurt)

2 large eggs

1 tbsp quality honey

2 tsp vanilla extract

¼ cup reduced-fat milk

Confectioners' sugar for garnish

Seasonal fruit (used here: 2 cups pitted cherries, plus 2 ripe nectarines, thinly sliced)

Honey Simple Syrup

1 cup quality honey

1 cup water

¼ tsp lime juice

Instructions

In a large baking dish (14-by-10 like this one, for example), do a quick test to see how many challah bread slices can fit in one layer without overlapping.

Now, using 1 tbsp soft butter, butter the bread on one side, and arrange in the prepared baking dish, buttered-side down.

Tear more bread, enough to fill any open spaces. Butter the torn pieces with the remaining soft butter, and fit them into open corners and cervices.

Make the custard. In a large bowl, whisk together the yogurt, eggs, honey, and vanilla. Pour over the challah; coat evenly using a spatula, and pull a few slices up to let the custard underneath.

Cover and refrigerate overnight.

In the morning, preheat the oven to 350 degrees F, and place an oven rack in the upper third.

Dot the challah all over with the cold butter, then pour ¼ cup milk all over.

Bake, uncovered, for about 30 minutes, or until the custard is set and the challah is almost firm to the touch. Flip on the broiler and broil for 2 minutes, watching carefully, until the top is golden brown.

While challah French toast is baking, make the honey simple syrup. In a small saucepan, combine honey and water. Bring to a boil over medium-high heat, stirring occasionally. Lower heat to simmer for about 20 minutes. Remove from heat and let cool to lukewarm. Stir in the lime juice.

To serve the baked challah bread French toast, sprinkle confectioners' sugar and top with your favorite fruit (we used pitted cherries and nectarines). Serve honey simple syrup next to it allowing everyone to help themselves to as much or as little syrup as they like. Enjoy!

#427. PUMPKIN GREEK YOGURT PARFAIT

Ready in about: 5 mins | serve: 6 | Nutritional value: Cal: 102g; Protein: 0.8g; Fat: 1.5g; Fiber: 0.6g; Carb: 15.6g

Ingredients

1 15-oz can pumpkin puree (or scant 2 cups homemade pumpkin puree)

1 ¼ cup low-fat Greek yogurt

3-4 Tbsp mascarpone cheese

1 tsp vanilla extract

2 tbsp molasses, more for garnish

2 ½ tbsp brown sugar

1 ½-2 tsp ground cinnamon

Pinch of nutmeg

Chocolate chips for garnish

Chopped hazelnuts or walnuts for garnish

Instructions

Place the pumpkin puree, Greek yogurt and the remaining ingredients, except the chocolate chips and nuts, in a large mixing bowl. Using a hand electric mixer or a whisk, mix together until you reach a smooth consistency.

Give it a taste and adjust flavor to your liking (add a bit of molasses or brown sugar to sweeten some more, for example. Or adjust the spices if you want more cinnamon or nutmeg.) Mix again to combine.

Transfer the pumpkin-yogurt mixture to small (3-oz) serving goblets or small mason jars. Cover and refrigerate for 30 minutes or overnight.

When ready to serve, top each with a drizzle of molasses, chocolate chips and chopped hazelnuts or walnuts. Enjoy!

#428. POACHED EGGS CAPRESE

Ready in about: 20 mins | serve: 2 | Nutritional value:
Cal: 482g; Protein: 33.3g; Fat: 25.9g; Fiber: g; Carb:
31.7g

<u>Ingredients</u>

1 tbsp distilled white vinegar

2 tsp salt

4 eggs

2 English muffins, split

4 (1 ounce) slices mozzarella cheese

1 tomato, thickly sliced

4 teaspoons pesto salt to taste

Directions

Fill a large saucepan with 2 to 3 inches of water and bring to a boil over high heat. Reduce the heat to medium-low, pour in the vinegar and 2 teaspoons of salt, and keep the water at a gentle simmer.

While waiting for the water to simmer, place a slice of mozzarella cheese and a thick slice of tomato onto each English muffin half, and toast in a toaster oven until the cheese softens and the English muffin has toasted, about 5 minutes.

Crack an egg into a small bowl. Holding the bowl just above the surface of the water, gently slip the egg into the simmering water. Repeat with the remaining eggs. Poach the eggs until the whites are firm and the yolks have thickened but are not hard, 2 1/2 to 3 minutes. Remove the eggs from the water with a slotted spoon, and dab on a kitchen towel to remove excess water.

To assemble, place a poached egg on top of each English muffin. Spoon a teaspoon of pesto sauce onto each egg and sprinkle with salt to taste.

#429. RASPBERRY CLAFOUTIS RECIPE

Ready in about: 35 mins | serve: 6| Nutritional value: Cal: 135g; Protein: 5.8g; Fat: 3.9g; Fiber: 4.1g; Carb: 33.5g

Equipment

Ceramic Baking Dish

Ingredients

Unsalted butter for baking dish

3 cups (350 grams) raspberries

½ cup plus 1 tablespoon granulated sugar divided

1 tsp dried lavender buds (optional)

½ cup (120 millilitres) whole milk

½ cup (114 grams) crème fraiche, more for serving (optional)

4 large eggs

Pinch salt

⅓ cup (43 grams) all-purpose flour

Confectioners' sugar for serving

Instructions

Heat the oven to 375 degrees F. Butter a 9-inch ceramic baking dish, or a 2-quart gratin dish, or a 9-inch cake pan.

In a medium bowl, toss the raspberries with 1 tbsp sugar. Let them sit while you prepare the remaining ingredients

In a food processor or blender, combine the remaining ½ cup sugar with the lavender; process until the lavender is mostly ground, about 2 minutes. Then pour the milk, crème fraiche, eggs, and salt, and process to combine. Add the flour and pulse just to combine.

Arrange the sugared berries in the prepared baking dish, then pour the egg mixture over them. Bake until the cake is golden and the center springs back when lightly touched, about 35 minutes.

Transfer the baking dish to a wire rack and let the cake cook for at least 15 minutes before serving. Then dust it with confectioners' sugar, slice it, and serve it with a dollop of whipped crème fraiche if you like (I used Greek yogurt to serve along).

#430. ROASTED PEACHES AND ORANGE WHIPPED GREEK YOGURT CROSTINI

Ready in about: 30 mins | serve: 10 | Nutritional value: Cal: 200g; Protein: 4.2g; Fat: 8.5g; Fiber: 3.4g; Carb: 28.4g

Ingredients

⅓ cup Greek yogurt
6 oz cream cheese, softened
zest of one orange, about 1 heaping tbsp

⅓ cup sugar
Pinch ground nutmeg
Pinch ground cinnamon
3 peaches, cored and sliced into thin wedges
3 tbsp orange juice
8-10 crostini, French baguette slices, toasted
¼ cup roughly chopped pecan halves
Honey to drizzle

Instructions

In a food processor, blend the Greek yogurt, cream cheese, orange zest, sugar, nutmeg and cinnamon. Run the processor until the mixture is well blended and fluffy. Place the whipped Greek yogurt mixture in a bowl. Cover and refrigerate for 1 hour or until ready to use.
Preheat the oven to 425 degrees F.
Toss the peaches with the orange juice in a bowl. Lightly pat the peaches dry and place them on a baking sheet lined with parchment paper. Bake in the 425-degree F-heated oven for 20-25 minutes.
When ready, generously spread the whipped Greek yogurt mixture over the toasted crostini/ French baguette slices. Top with the chopped pecans and two slices of the roasted peaches. Drizzle a little honey over each crostino. Enjoy!

#431. SUMMER FRUIT COMPOTE RECIPE

Ready in about: 15 mins | serve: 4, Makes 4 toasts|
Nutritional value: Cal: 167g; Protein: 23.5g; Fat: 10.9g;
Fiber: 0g; Carb: 10.9g

Ingredients

1 lb peaches (3 to 4 peaches), halved, pitted, then thinly sliced

1 lb cherries, pitted and halved

1 tsp ground cinnamon

2 cups red wine like an inexpensive Merlot

¾ cup cane sugar

1 ½ cup plain fat-free Greek yogurt

1 tsp vanilla extract

Quality honey, to your liking

Instructions

Place sliced peaches and cherries in a large mixing bowl. Sprinkle with cinnamon. Toss. Set aside.

Combine wine and sugar in a saucepan. Heat on high for 5 minutes until sugar dissolves fully.

Pour hot wine syrup over fruit. Cover and set aside for 1 hour to cool. Discard a good portion of syrup, pouring a little in a cup for use later.

In a small bowl, combine the Greek yogurt, vanilla extract, and honey. Mix.

Serve wine-poached fruit with a little of the poaching syrup and a dollop of the honeyed Greek yogurt. Enjoy!

#432. SPINACH FETA BREAKFAST WRAPS

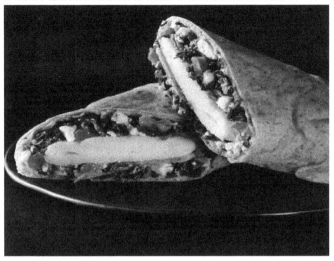

Ready in about: 20 mins | serve: 4 | Nutritional value: Cal: 543g; Protein: 28.1g; Fat: 27.0g; Fiber: 4.4g; Carb: 46.5g

Ingredients

10 large eggs

1/2-pound (about 5 cups) baby spinach

4 whole-wheat tortillas (about 9 inches in diameter, burrito-sized)

1/2-pint cherry or grape tomatoes, halved

4 ounces feta cheese, crumbled

Butter or olive oil

Salt

Pepper

Instructions

In a large bowl, whisk the eggs until the whites and yolks are completely combined. Place a large skillet over medium heat and add enough butter or olive oil to coat the bottom. When the butter is melted or the oil is hot, pour in the eggs and stir occasionally until the eggs are cooked. Stir in a pinch of salt and a generous amount of black pepper, then transfer to a large plate to cool to room temperature.

Rinse or wipe down the skillet, place it back over medium heat, and add another pat of butter or oil. Add the spinach and cook, stirring often, until the spinach is just wilted. Spread the cooked spinach on another large plate to cool to room temperature.

Arrange a tortilla on a work surface. Add about a quarter each of the eggs, spinach, tomatoes, and feta down the middle of the tortilla and tightly wrap (see How To Wrap a Burrito). Repeat with the remaining three tortillas. Place the wraps in a gallon zip-top bag and freeze until ready to eat. If freezing for more than a week, wrap the burritos in aluminum foil to prevent freezer burn. To reheat, microwave on high for 2 minutes.

#433. SPANISH TORTILLA RECIPE

Ready in about: 25 mins | serve: 6 | Nutritional value: Cal: 381g; Protein: 12g; Fat: 5.3g; Fiber: 2.1g; Carb: 23.5g

Ingredients

10 medium eggs

Salt

1 tsp sweet Spanish paprika, optional

1 cup extra virgin olive oil

1 ½ lb russet potatoes (or 2 to 3 russet potatoes), peeled, halved and sliced cross-wise

1 large yellow onion, peeled, halved and sliced cross-wise

4 scallions, trimmed, chopped (both white and green portions)

Instructions

In a big bowl, whisk together the eggs, salt, and paprika. Set aside for now.

Prepare a 10-inch oven-proof nonstick skillet or a well-seasoned cast iron skillet. Heat the olive oil in the skillet over medium-high heat until shimmering but not smoking.

Add the potatoes, onions, and scallions to the oil (at first, they won't all seem to fit, but with a little stirring, they'll compress as they cook). Lower the heat immediately to medium-low and watch to control the heat and make sure it continues to gently bubble. Cook for 25 minutes, stirring occasionally, until the potatoes are very tender.

Use a heat-safe strainer over a heat-safe bowl to drain the olive oil (reserve the oil aside for now).

Season the potatoes well with kosher salt and add them to the egg mixture in the bowl.

Turn the oven broiler on.

In the skillet, heat 3 tablespoons of the reserved olive oil over medium heat. Pour in the egg and potato mixture, and gently press to even out the top. Reduce the heat to medium-low. Cook until you see the edges of the omelet begin to set and firm up then put the pan under the broiler to finish cooking. Broil for about 5 minutes, watching carefully until the eggs are cooked through and the top of the omelet browns slightly (see notes if you prefer to finish cooking on stovetop).

Allow the tortilla a few minutes before serving.

To serve, invert the tortilla onto a large serving platter (you may need to loosen the edges using a spatula). Cut into 6 slices and serve.

#434. SPINACH AND ARTICHOKE FRITTATA

Ready in about: 25 mins | serve: 4 -6 | Nutritional value: Cal: 316g; Protein: 17.9g; Fat: 25.9g; Fiber: 2.3g; Carb: 6.4g

Ingredients

10 large eggs

1/2 cup full-fat sour cream

1 tbsp Dijon mustard

1 tsp kosher salt

1/4 teaspoon freshly ground black pepper

1 cup grated Parmesan cheese (about 3 ounces), divided

2 tablespoons olive oil

About 14 ounces marinated artichoke hearts, drained, patted dry, and quartered

5 ounces baby spinach (about 5 packed cups)

2 cloves garlic, minced

Instructions

Arrange a rack in the middle of the oven and heat to 400°F.

Place the eggs, sour cream, mustard, salt, pepper and 1/2 cup of the Parmesan in a large bowl and whisk to combine; set aside.

Heat the oil in a 10-inch cast iron or oven-safe nonstick skillet over medium heat until shimmering. Add the artichokes in a single layer and cook, stirring occasionally, until lightly browned, 6 to 8 minutes. Add the spinach and garlic, and toss until the spinach is wilted and almost all of the liquid is evaporated, about 2 minutes.

Spread everything into an even layer. Pour the egg mixture over the vegetables. Sprinkle with the remaining 1/2 cup Parmesan. Tilt the pan to make sure the eggs settle evenly over all the vegetables. Cook undisturbed until the eggs at the edges of the pan begin to set, 2 to 3 minutes.

Bake until the eggs are completely set, 12 to 15 minutes. To check, cut a small slit in the center of the frittata. If raw eggs run into the cut, bake for another few minutes. Cool in the pan for 5 minutes, then slice into wedges and serve warm.

#435. SHAKSHUKA

Ready in about: 30 mins | serve: 4 to 6| Nutritional value: Cal: 146g; Protein: 7.9g; Fat: 9.7g; Fiber: 3.0g; Carb: 7.8g

Ingredients

1 (28-ounce) can whole peeled tomatoes

2 tbsp olive oil

1 small yellow onion, finely chopped

2 tbsp tomato paste

1 tbsp harissa

3 cloves garlic, minced

1 tsp ground cumin

1/2 tsp kosher salt

6 large eggs

1/4 cup loosely packed chopped fresh cilantro leaves and tender stems

2 ounces feta cheese, crumbled (about 1/2 cup, optional)

Crusty bread or pita, for serving (optional)

Equipment

10- or 12-inch skillet with lid

Instructions

Crush the tomatoes. Pour the tomatoes and their juices into a large bowl. Carefully crush with your hands into bite-sized pieces; set aside.

Sauté the aromatics. Heat the oil in a 10- or 12-inch skillet over medium heat until shimmering. Add the onion and sauté until translucent and softened, 5 to 6 minutes. Add the tomato paste, harissa, garlic, cumin, and salt, and sauté until fragrant, about 1 minute.

Simmer the tomato sauce for 10 minutes. Add the tomatoes and bring to a simmer. Simmer gently until the sauce has thickened slightly, about 10 minutes.

Crack the eggs into the sauce. Remove the skillet from the heat. Make 6 small wells in the sauce. Crack an egg into each well.

Spoon some sauce over the egg whites. Gently spoon a bit of sauce over the egg whites, leaving the yolks exposed (this will help the whites cook faster so they set before the yolks). Cover and return the skillet to medium-low heat.

Cook the eggs 8 to 12 minutes. Cook, rotating the pan as needed so that the eggs cook evenly, until the whites are set and the yolks are to your desired doneness, 8 to 12 minutes (check on it a few times). The eggs should still jiggle in the centers when you gently shake the pan.

Finish with cilantro and cheese. Remove from the heat. Sprinkle with the cilantro and feta, if using, and serve with bread or pita if desired.

#436. SMASHED EGG TOASTS WITH HERBY LEMON YOGURT

Ready in about: 15 mins | serve: 4, Makes 4 toasts|
Nutritional value: Cal: 437g; Protein: 23.5g; Fat: 35.5g;
Fiber: 0.6g; Carb: 7.4g

Ingredients

8 large eggs

1 clove garlic

1 medium lemon

2 tbsp finely chopped fresh basil leaves, plus more for garnish

2 tbsp finely chopped fresh dill, plus more for garnish

2 tbsp finely chopped fresh chives, plus more for garnish

2 cups plain Greek yogurt

2 tbsp extra-virgin olive oil, plus more for drizzling

3/4 tsp kosher salt, plus more for sprinkling

1/2 tsp freshly ground black pepper, plus more for sprinkling

4 large slices country or sourdough bread (about 1-inch thick)

4 tbsp unsalted butter, divided

Instructions

Fill a large pot with about 5 inches of water and bring to a rolling boil over high heat; fill a large bowl with cold water and ice. Lower the heat until the water is at a rapid simmer. Gently lower 8 large eggs into the water one at a time. Boil for exactly 6 minutes and 30 seconds. Using a slotted spoon, transfer the eggs to the ice bath. Let sit in the ice bath for 2 minutes, then peel the eggs under running water and set them aside.

Prepare the following, adding them to a medium bowl: Mince 1 garlic clove. Finely grate the zest 1 medium lemon, then juice the lemon. Finely chop until you have 2 tablespoons fresh basil leaves, 2 tablespoons fresh dill, and 2 tablespoons fresh chives. Add 2 cups Greek yogurt, 2 tablespoons extra-virgin olive oil, 3/4 teaspoon kosher salt, and 1/2 teaspoon black pepper. Stir to combine.

Cut 4 (1-inch thick) slices crusty bread. Melt 2 tablespoons unsalted butter in a large skillet over medium heat. Add 2 of the slices and cook until golden brown and crisp, about 2 minutes per side. Transfer to a large platter. Repeat with the remaining 2 tablespoons unsalted butter and bread.

Spread the yogurt mixture on the bread, then top each toast with 2 of the eggs. Using the back of a spoon, gently smash the eggs. Sprinkle with more kosher salt, black pepper, and herbs, and drizzle with more olive oil.

#437. SIMPLE APPLE GALETTE RECIPE WITH BUTTER RUM SYRUP

Ready in about: 1 hour 20 minutes | serve: 4 -6 | Nutritional value: Cal: 642g; Protein: 7.7g; Fat: 32.3g; Fiber: 6.3g; Carb: 79.9g
Ingredients

For the Galette Dough
2 c. all-purpose flour
½ c. semolina flour (or corn flour)
1 tsp sugar
½ tsp salt
12 tbsp unsalted butter, cut into small cubes
½ c. ice water
For the Apple Topping
2 large baking apples (Pink Lady, for example), peeled, cut, cored and sliced into ¼-inch slices
½ c. spiced rum
2 tbsp brown sugar
½ tsp ground cinnamon
½ tsp ground nutmeg
1 egg, beaten with 1 tbsp water (egg wash)
2 tbsp unsalted butter, cut into small cubes
For the Butter Rum Syrup
1 c. brown sugar
¾ c. water
2 tbsp butter
½ c. spiced rum

Instructions

Begin by making the basic galette dough. In a bowl, whisk together the all-purpose flour, semolina flour, sugar and salt. Add ½ of the butter and work the dough with your hand until the mixture resembles coarse meal. Add the remaining butter and continue to work the dough (the largest piece of butter should be pea-size). Now add the water and mix with your hands until the dough comes together. Flatten the dough into a disc and warp it with plastic. Refrigerate for at least 30 minutes. Meanwhile, preheat the oven to 400 degrees F, and begin to prepare the apple topping.

Place the apple slices in a deep dish. Pour the rum on top and let it rest for 15 minutes, then add the sugar, cinnamon and nutmeg.

When ready, with a rolling pin, roll the dough out onto a lightly floured surface to form a large rectangle. Carefully transfer the dough to a large baking sheet lined with parchment paper.

Discard the rum in which the apples were soaking. Arrange the apple slices in two overlapping rows on the dough (see photo) leaving about 1-inch boarder. Fold the excess dough over the apple topping creating a frame. Brush the dough frame with the egg wash. Finally, dot the top of the apple topping with the butter cubes. Place the galette in the 400 F degree-heated oven and bake for 30 minutes. Rotate the baking sheet then bake for 30 more minutes until the pie crust is golden brown. (To achieve the charred look of the apple topping, broil ever so briefly watching carefully to avoid burning).

Remove the galette from the oven. Let it cool before slicing.

While the galette is cooling, prepare the butter rum syrup. In a sauce pan, combine the brown sugar, water and butter over medium heat. Cook for 1-2 minutes until the sugar has completely dissolved and the butter melted. Reduce the heat to low and add the rum. Let simmer for 2 more minutes. Remove from heat and use warm on top of the apple galette. Enjoy!

#438. SIMPLE GREEN JUICE RECIPE

Ready in about: 15 mins | serve: 2| Nutritional value:
Cal: 92g; Protein: 2.8g; Fat: 0.8g; Fiber: 6.2g; Carb: 21g

Ingredients

1 bunch kale (about 5 oz)

1-inch piece fresh ginger, peeled

1 Granny smith apple (or any large apple)

5 celery stalks, ends trimmed

½ large English cucumber

Handful fresh parsley (about 1 oz)

Instructions

Wash and prep the vegetables. I like to cut them in large chunks.

Juice in the order listed (or add them to a blender and blend on high.)

If you used a juicer, simply pour the green juice into glasses and enjoy immediately. If you used a blender, the juice will be thicker. You can pour it through a fine mesh sieve, and using the back of a spoon, press the pulp into the sieve to extract as much liquid as possible. Pour the strained juice into glasses and enjoy!

#439. TAHINI BANANA DATE SHAKES

Ready in about: 5 mins | serve: 3 | Nutritional value:
Cal: 100g; Protein: 6.5g; Fat: 0.5g; Fiber: 6.5g; Carb:
21.5g

Ingredients

2 frozen bananas, sliced

4 pitted Medjool dates (if they're too big, you can chop
them up a bit.)

¼ cup tahini (I used Sodom tahini)

¼ cup crushed ice

1 ½ cups unsweetened almond milk

Pinch ground cinnamon, more for later

Instructions

Place the sliced frozen bananas in your blender, add the remaining ingredients. Run blender until you achieve a smooth and creamy shake.

Transfer the banana date shakes to serving cups and add pinch more ground cinnamon on top. Enjoy!

#440. VEGETARIAN EGG CASSEROLE

Ready in about: 50 mins | serve: 12 | Nutritional value: Cal: 126g; Protein: 7g; Fat: 6.3g; Fiber: 7.6g; Carb: 11.5g

<u>Ingredients</u>

7 to 8 large eggs

1 ½ cups milk (I used 2% milk)

½ tsp baking powder

Kosher salt and black pepper

1 tsp dry oregano

1 tsp sweet paprika

¼ tsp nutmeg

3 slices bread (toast), cut into ½ inch pieces (use whole grain bread for Mediterranean diet option)

2 shallots, thinly sliced

1 tomato, small diced

3 oz sliced mushrooms (any kind), optional

4 oz artichoke hearts from a can, drained and quartered

2 oz pitted kalamata olives, sliced

2 to 3 oz crumbled feta cheese

1 oz chopped fresh parsley (about 1 cup loosely packed)

Extra virgin olive oil (I used Private Reserve Greek olive oil)

1 bell pepper (any color), sliced into rounds

Instructions

Heat oven to 375 degrees F and adjust an oven rack to the middle

In a large mixing bowl, whisk together the eggs, milk, baking powder, salt, pepper, and spices.

To the egg mixture, add the bread pieces, shallots, tomatoes, mushrooms, artichoke hearts, kalamata olives, and parsley. Mix until everything is well combined.

Lightly brush a 9" x 13" casserole dish with extra virgin olive oil. Transfer the egg and vegetable mixture into the casserole dish and spread evenly. Arrange the bell pepper slices on top.

Place the egg casserole on the middle rack of your heated oven and bake for about 35 to 45 minutes or until the eggs are cooked through and the center of the casserole looks firm (test with a toothpick or a fork).

#441. ZA'ATAR MANAQISH RECIPE

Ready in about: 2 hrs. and 38 mins| serve: 8 | Nutritional value: Cal: 306g; Protein: 5.5g; Fat: 14.7g; Fiber: 2.3g; Carb: 38.2g

Ingredients

for dough

1 cup lukewarm water
½ tsp sugar
2 ¼ tsp active dry yeast (one package active dry yeast)
3 cups unbleached all-purpose flour, more for dusting
1 tsp salt
2 tbsp Private Reserve extra virgin olive oil

for za'atar topping

7 to 8 tbsp quality Za'atar spice
½ cup Private Reserve extra virgin olive oil
Serve with

Fresh garden vegetables (tomato, cucumbers, radish)
Olives
Homemade labneh or feta cheese (omit if vegan)

Instructions

In a small bowl, combine water, sugar and yeast. Set aside for 10 minutes to foam.
Make the dough. In a large mixing bowl, combine flour, salt, and olive oil. Work the mixture with your hands. Now, make a well in the middle and pour in the yeast and water mixture. Stir until soft dough forms.

Turn dough onto a lightly floured surface and knead for 10 minutes or until dough is elastic, smooth, and no longer sticky (as you knead, if dough is too sticky for you, you can sprinkle just a tiny bit of flour to help it). Form dough into a ball and place in a lightly oiled mixing bowl. Cover with damp cloth and place in a warm spot (inside a warmed but turned-off oven is a good place). Leave to rise for 1 hour and 30 minutes. Punch dough down. Knead briefly and form into 8 small balls. Arrange on lightly floured surface, cover again and leave to rise another 30 minutes.

Prepare the za'atar topping. While dough is rising, mix together the za'atar spice and olive oil in a bowl.

Preheat the oven to 400 degrees F. Place a large baking sheet in oven while heating.

Form za'atar manaqish. Lightly oil the heated baking sheet and set near you. Flatten the dough into small discs about 5 inches in diameter. With your fingertips, make indentations in discs and add about 1 tbsp za'atar topping in the middle of each disc, leave a narrow boarder around. Arrange discs in prepared oiled baking sheet (use two sheets if needed, do not crowd the manaqish).

Bake in 400 degrees F heated-oven for 7 to 8 minutes or until the dough is slightly browned on bottom and edges (za'atar topping will remain liquidly at this point).

Remove from heat and let sit for 5 minutes or so, the topping will dry and settle into dough.

Serve za'atar manaqish warm or at room temperature with assorted vegetables, olives, feta cheese, or homemade labneh.

MEDITERRANEAN SOUP RECIPES.

#442. ARBORIO RICE AND WHITE BEAN SOUP

Ready in about: 30 mins / serving: 4

Nutrition facts: Cal: 303g; fat: 6g; Carb: 52g; fiber: 5g; protein: 9g

Ingredients
1 tbsp olive oil
3 garlic cloves, minced
3/4 cup uncooked arborio rice
1 carton (32 ounces) vegetable broth
3/4 tsp dried basil
1/2 tsp dried thyme
1/4 tsp dried oregano
1 package (16 ounces) frozen broccoli-cauliflower blend
1 can (15 ounces) cannellini beans, rinsed and drained
2 cups fresh baby spinach
Lemon wedges, optional

Instruction

In a large saucepan, heat oil over medium heat; saute garlic 1 minute. Add rice; cook and stir 2 minutes. Stir in broth and herbs; bring to a boil. Reduce heat; simmer, covered, until rice is al dente, about 10 minutes. Stir in frozen vegetables and beans; cook, covered, over medium heat until heated through and rice is tender, 8-10 minutes, stirring occasionally. Stir in spinach until wilted. If desired, serve with lemon wedges.

#443. BEAN COUNTER CHOWDER

Ready in about: 30 mins / serving: 8

Nutrition facts: Cal: 196g; fat: 3g; Carb: 33g; fiber: 5g; protein: 28g

Ingredients
1/2 cup chopped onion
1 tbsp canola oil

2 garlic cloves, minced
1 medium tomato, chopped
2 cans (14-1/2 ounces each) chicken or vegetable broth
1-3/4 cups water
1/2 tsp each dried basil, oregano and celery flakes
1/4 tsp pepper
3 cans (15-1/2 ounces each) great northern beans, rinsed
and drained
1 cup uncooked elbow macaroni
1 tbsp minced parsley

Instruction

In a large saucepan, saute onion in oil until tender; Add
garlic; cook 1 minute longer. Add the tomato; simmer
for 5 minutes. Add the broth, water and seasonings.
Bring to a boil; cook for 5 minutes. Add beans and
macaroni; return to a boil.
Reduce heat; simmer, uncovered, until macaroni is
tender, about 15 minutes. Sprinkle with parsley.

#444. BROCCOLI CHEESE SOUP

Ready in about: 20 mins / serving: 4

Nutrition facts: Cal: 290g; fat: 7g; Carb: 50g; fiber: 8g; protein: 19g

<u>Ingredients</u>
1-1/2 cups chopped onions
2 tbsp butter
6 cups hot water
6 chicken bouillon cubes
1/4 tsp garlic powder
8 ounces uncooked pasta
2 tsp salt
6 cups frozen chopped broccoli
6 cups milk
1-pound process cheese (Velveeta), cubed

Instruction

In a Dutch oven or soup kettle, saute onion in butter until tender. Add the water, bouillon and garlic powder; bring to a boil. Stir until bouillon is dissolved. Add pasta and salt; cook and stir for 3 minutes.

Add broccoli; cook and stir for 3-4 minutes or until pasta is tender. Add milk and cheese; cook and stir over low heat until cheese is melted.

#445. BEEF AND VEGETABLE SOUP

Ready in about: 40 mins / serving: 6

Nutrition facts: Cal: 240g; fat: 7g, 27g; Carb: 32g; 7g fiber: 7g; protein: 12g.

Ingredients

1 medium onion (about 1 1/2 cup chopped)

3 garlic cloves

2 large carrots

2 celery stalks

1-pound lean ground beef (95% lean)

2 tbsp tomato paste

2 tsp Italian seasoning

3 cups beef broth

1 can fire roasted diced tomatoes (14.5 oz. per can)

1 can cannellini beans (15 oz. per can)

1/4 crushed red pepper flakes (optional, more if desired)

8 ounces Swiss chard (4 cups chopped)

1/2 tsp salt (or more to taste)

1/4 tsp pepper (or more to taste)

1/2 cup grated parmesan cheese

Instruction

Chop onion and garlic. Peel and chop carrots, and chop celery. Set carrots and celery aside.
Saute beef and onion in a Dutch oven over medium-high heat, stirring frequently to break up meat, until beef is cooked through and onion is translucent, 6 minutes. Add tomato paste, garlic, and Italian seasoning and cook, stirring constantly, until fragrant, 45 seconds. (Pro tip: use lean ground beef so the soup won't be greasy.)

Add broth, tomatoes, carrots, and celery to pot. Rinse and drain cannellini beans and stir them into pot. Bring soup to a simmer over high heat, cover, reduce heat to low, and simmer until vegetables are tender, 15 minutes. Meanwhile, prepare chard.

#446. CREAMY WHITE CHILI

Ready in about: 2 hrs. 38 mins| serve: 7 | Nutritional value: Cal: 334g; Protein: 22g; Fat: 24g; Fiber: 22g; Carb: 7g

Ingredients

1-pound boneless skinless chicken breasts, cut into 1/2-inch cubes

1 medium onion, chopped

1-1/2 tsp garlic powder

1 tbsp canola oil

2 cans (15-1/2 ounces each) great northern beans, rinsed and drained

1 can (14-1/2 ounces) chicken broth

2 cans (4 ounces each) chopped green chiles

1 tsp salt

1 tsp ground cumin

1 tsp dried oregano

1/2 tsp pepper

1/4 tsp cayenne pepper

1 cup sour cream

1/2 cup heavy whipping cream

Tortilla chips, optional

Shredded cheddar cheese, optional

Sliced seeded jalapeno pepper, optional

Instruction

In a large saucepan, saute the chicken, onion and garlic powder in oil until chicken is no longer pink. Add the beans, broth, chiles and seasonings. Bring to a boil. Reduce heat; simmer, uncovered, for 30 minutes.

Remove from the heat; stir in sour cream and cream. If desired, top with tortilla chips, cheese and jalapenos.

#447. CHICKEN LEEK SOUP WITH WHITE WINE

Ready in about: 1hr. 20 mins| serve: 6 | Nutritional value: Cal: 180g; Protein: 9g; Fat: 7g; Fiber: 7g; Carb: 4g

Ingredients

1/2 cup extra virgin olive oil

2 pounds chicken breast, cut into bite-sized pieces

1 large leek, cut into thin rounds

4 green onions (scallions), chopped

4 celery sticks, chopped

1 small cabbage, cut into thick slices

1 cup white wine

Salt and pepper, to taste

1/2 teaspoon paprika

Pinch of nutmeg

3 cups water

Instructions

In a deep pot, heat the olive oil. Add the chicken and sauté until cooked on the outside. Add the leeks, green onions, and celery. Sauté for 1 minute.

Add cabbage and sauté for a few minutes until fork tender. Add wine, salt, pepper, paprika, nutmeg and water. Mix well.

Cook on low heat for 45 minutes.

#448. CIOPPINO-STYLE SOUP

Ready in about: 1hr. 20 min. / serving: 6

Nutrition facts: Cal: 208g; fat: 6g; Carb: 16g; fiber: 27g; protein: 21g

Ingredients
2 tbsp olive oil
2 medium red onions, chopped
3 garlic cloves, minced
1 can (28 ounces) no-salt-added crushed tomatoes
1 carton (32 ounces) vegetable stock
1 cup dry red wine
1-1/2 tsp Italian seasoning
1/2 tsp pepper
1/2 tsp crushed red pepper flakes, optional
6 ounces uncooked shrimp (31-40 per pound), peeled and deveined
1 can (6 ounces) lump crabmeat, drained
2 cod fillets (6 ounces each), cut into 1-inch pieces
1/3 cup chopped fresh parsley
Shredded Parmesan cheese, optional

Instruction
In a 6-qt. stockpot, heat oil over medium heat. Add onions; cook and stir 4-6 minutes or until tender. Add garlic; cook 1 minute longer. Add tomatoes, stock, wine, Italian seasoning and pepper; stir in pepper flakes if desired. Bring to a boil. Reduce heat; simmer, covered, 1 hour to allow flavors to blend.
Add shrimp, crab, cod and parsley; cook until shrimp turn pink and fish just begins to flake easily with a fork,

3-5 minutes longer. If desired, top each serving with cheese.

#449. CREAM OF LENTIL SOUP

Ready in about: 20 mins / serving: 10

Nutrition facts: Cal: 344g; fat: 20g; Carb: 30g; fiber: 5g; protein: 13g

Ingredients
6 cups reduced-sodium chicken broth or vegetable broth, divided
2 cups dried lentils, rinsed
1 bay leaf
1 whole clove
1 medium red onion, chopped
2 celery ribs, chopped
2 tbsp butter
2 medium carrots, chopped
1 tsp salt

1 tsp sugar
1/2 tsp curry powder
1/8 tsp pepper
2 garlic cloves, minced
3 cups coarsely chopped fresh spinach
2 cups heavy whipping cream
1 tbsp lemon juice
1/3 cup minced fresh parsley

Instruction

In a large saucepan, combine the 4 cups of broth, lentils, bay leaf and clove. Bring to a boil. Reduce heat; cover and simmer until lentils are tender, 25-30 minutes. Meanwhile, in a Dutch oven, saute onion and celery in butter until crisp-tender. Add the carrots, salt, sugar, curry powder and pepper; saute until vegetables are tender, 2-3 minutes longer . Add garlic; cook for 1 minute.

Drain lentils; discard broth, bay leaf and clove. Add lentils to vegetable mixture. Stir in the spinach, remaining 2 cups broth, cream, lemon juice and parsley; cook over low heat until heated through and spinach is wilted.

#450. CASSOULET FOR THE GANG

Ready in about: 40 mins / serving: 10

Nutrition facts: Cal: 316g; fat: 5g; Carb: 40g; fiber: 6g; protein: 25g

Ingredients
1-pound pork tenderloin, cut into 1/2-inch pieces
1-pound smoked turkey kielbasa, cut into 1/2-inch pieces
1 asp olive oil
3 medium carrots, chopped
1 large onion, cut into wedges
4 garlic cloves, minced
2 cans (14-1/2 ounces each) no-salt-added stewed tomatoes, cut up
1 can (14-1/2 ounces) reduced-sodium chicken broth
3 tsp herbs de Provence
1-1/2 tsp garlic powder
1-1/2 tsp dried basil

1/2 tsp dried oregano
1/4 tsp pepper
4 cans (15-1/2 ounces each) great northern beans, rinsed
and drained, divided
3/4 cup white wine or additional chicken broth, divided

Instruction

In a Dutch oven coated with cooking spray, saute pork
and kielbasa in oil until lightly browned; drain. Add
carrots and onion; saute 4 minutes longer. Add garlic;
cook for 1 minute longer. Stir in the tomatoes, broth and
seasonings. Bring to a boil. Reduce heat; cover and
simmer for 10 minutes.

Place 1 can of beans in a food processor; add 1/4 cup
wine. Cover and process until pureed. Stir into meat
mixture. Stir in the remaining beans and wine. Bring to
a boil. Reduce heat; simmer, uncovered, for 8-10
minutes or until meat and vegetables are tender.

Freeze option: Freeze cooled cassoulet in freezer
containers. To use, partially thaw in refrigerator
overnight. Heat through in a saucepan, stirring
occasionally and adding a little broth or water if
necessary.

CPSIA information can be obtained
at www.ICGtesting.com
Printed in the USA
BVHW061125040521
606417BV00006B/1170